To my wife Ann

More Thoughts Along the Way

More Thoughts Along the Way

by

Peter Hutley

Wintershall Press
London

© Peter Hutley 2003

First Published in 2003 by
Wintershall Press
London

All rights reserved.
Unauthorised duplication contravenes existing laws.

British Library Cataloguing in Publication Data.
A Catalogue record for this book is available from the British Library

ISBN 0-9545161-0-9

Contents

		Page
1.	My Christian Karma Credo	1
2.	Alaskan Summer	4
3.	Barn Owls	6
4.	Battle	7
5.	Bethel	8
6.	Camera Time	9
7.	Big Bang and Us	10
8.	Our Life	13
9.	Jerusalem	14
10.	On Reading 'In the Footsteps of St. Paul'	16
11.	The Artist	17
12.	Reality	18
13.	Time Valuable	19
14.	Reflections	20
15.	Life is Short	22
16.	The Sensor of Compostela	23
17.	Waiting in Retribution	24
18.	World War and August	26
19.	Wales & Brecon	33
20.	The Australian Property Unit Trust (APUT)	36
20.	The Builder	37
21.	To Grandchildren - The World is Yours	38
22.	South Island, New Zealand	39
23.	That	41
24.	Rehearsals	42
25.	My Secret	43
26.	Ancient Oceans	44
27.	Spring Time 2002	46
28.	Michael's Speech	48
29.	Reflections on Spring	50
30.	My Life of Goodbyes	51
31.	Jesus Today	52
32.	God's Voice	53
33.	A Little History	54
34.	Future Peril	55
35.	Recollections	57
36.	A Little Prayer	59
37.	Santiago de Compostela	60
38.	To My Sons	62

My Christian Karma Credo

O Lord of all Spirits come to me today
that I may know your truth and light and, unseeing,
feel your presence beyond my worldly life,
and have your power and grace infuse my living soul,
and fill my heart.

The mysteries of space and endless time abound
and my own quest for spirit seems allied to them.
Are they all one and share the same neglect
of human comprehension?
Or are time and space a simple conundrum,
compared with faith and living soul?
One linked with lifetimes universe
and therefore still material,
the other of our God in deeper mystery riven.

So I did turn to Him to gain the answer to it all?
To simplify both time and space to terms
of human understanding.
And, in a flash, to comprehend it all -
if He would tell me.

Yet spirit is still for comprehension
but gives my mortal life dimension.
Greater than my body, brain and heart
I believe my encapsulated soul is,
on my departure, preserved to undergo
examination of my life
to render me wheat or chaff for long eternity.

That inner power that drives me to both love and sin
is in my soul, full charged with spirit, to which I
listen or at times discard.
For this essential fibre of my being, I control with
my free will,
I direct my soul and I hold responsibility for what I
do and must account for every moment of my life.

But redemption,
faith and trust are also graces that are given,
leading me unknowingly along my daily path.
An ordination that I must follow
and when I go against that natural route,
then I know the guilt, the sense of failure
that no earthly joy does compensate.

My heart, untaught, discerns the secret message of
my soul
that I know right from wrong in every sense
and therefore this is proof for me,
such glorious evidence,
that planted in my soul, my depth,
unknown, yet so truly there, is Godly presence,
as in all mankind does exist,
and, as in His likeness is my frame,
His spirit is within me too.
If in mortal years and earthly life,
I transcend to sin and grime
then I pull Him within me down
and that's immortal crime

for which I know I must one day account.
But redemption comes if my sorrow lasts
and grief for past times sin becomes sincere,
for that's the message in the Book and also deep
within my heart.

So with confidence I feel forgiveness will await,
my punishment will not last all time,
but some I know, will come
that I deserve, can bear and later in forgiveness live.

✿ ✿ ✿

Alaskan Summer at Quinahoc

In summer there, rare streaks of snow in valleys lie,
and jagged peaks, on blown cloud,
give way to sudden pebble strands.
Oxbows are born as rivers wash the fragile earth
and soft coasts erode their muddy shores
where tidal sea and rivers whirlpools cause.

In shallow sea sovereign salmon
penetrate the saltless river to its source,
then blush their silver lustre red,
for these great kings, by loyalty driven,
return to spawn new life
where they themselves were riven.

The dying snow, that rushing river makes,
is highway for chinook and chums, sockeye and char,
But each their distance keep, and are a pure breed,
glorious in their individualities.
And out of tundra: bright flame weed bursts
and, in its little summer, entwines wild strawberries
and caribou grow fat - lush milk their calves on arctic cream.

Big beaver slaps the water with his tail
and disciplines the young to faster work,
that lodges for long winter warmth
become complete before their world by ice is closed.
So all along the rivers edge, to measured height,

the summer alders trimmed to stubble size
and branches, through secret tunnels taken,
to musty domes of silent peace,
as winter food where new born beavers lie.

A shy giant stalks it all but with a bound,
a sweep, a splash, a triumphant bear a salmon strikes
and food for him converts to layered blubber,
under shiny fur and double skin.
His sharp cold eye means he knows us not
and shows his fear but there's no hate in him.

Soon now new snow a blanket forms,
on tundra's teeming life, that all may sleep,
in crevices beneath that mantle warm
and salmon fry wait out their turn to ocean dash,
when all does melt and come to life - reborn.

Barn Owls

Was it hissing? No sissing,
no that's not quite right,
it's a special sound of breathing
but rare, so rare it's unrecognisable:
to most.
But I recall in Vaud sleeping disgruntledly
'neath such a sound.
The children had said this is the owl's room.
They knew for after Chile
they had lived there in Swiss summer's heat
and early autumn mellowness.
They knew an owl asleep or waking.
Its breath, unknown to almost all,
is indescribable.
Not sweet, nor fearsome,
noticeable and having heard:
unforgettable.

A sound I cannot imitate,
it's old, like oceans,
and pre the modern world.
Maybe its God's sound,
for sure it's from no other known creature.
Let's hope our Barn Owls last out the winter.

Battle

They laid fearing to move,
awaiting bullets to lop into their limbs,
shells to shatter their eyes - explode their lungs -
knowing they'd die, longing to live
hating the killing but wanting to kill.

Many died, heaped up, some spread -
as death falls, different from life,
arms broken and thrown across legs,
torn and blown,
in pain that's not felt, as blood
just drips out,
that is death in the line.
An ache in the throat
that lasts for ever.

Shan States 1948

Bethel

How many names from the Holy Book
came to desperate men who claimed America as
theirs.
The name of Bethel so many times vibrates from
Alaska down to Louis.
But Bethel is but a mile or two from Jerusalem!
Where Jesus did proclaim that he would die for us.
Those gracious saints,
whose names enshrined those longing hopes,
possessed by all, that we could love like them.

✣ ✣ ✣

Camera Time and Ours

A camera can quicken up and some slow down,
to meet the pace our living eye can see.
Great skies and deciduous trees can, upon the screen,
unfold in moments
but take hours or months when seen by human eye
alone.
Flying wings and running legs when by camera slowed
reveal their shapeliness and moving speed.

But time for us is as God decides.
A century can be like a day just gone
and a moment last that all its joys and tinkling sounds
survive a lifetime in our human memory.

So that's the fluke of time.
The present is now, already past for some
or not here at all for those so fearful of the future.
Yet if we trust then every moment of our lives can last
for ever.
Is that eternity and faith the key?

Big Bang and Us

Driven from my head for now
are thoughts of love, eternal God and peace,
as scientific knowledge invades my mind
and time and distance define the facts
of universe, of life and mankind's origin.

They say that fifteen billion years ago,
a heavy sphere of elements exploded,
with a lingering sound
that even lasts through to to-day.
And from this bang the universe was thrown out
and every star and moon and planet burst.

But I must ask what existed before all that
and what or who did cause the Bang?
I now know, and don't we all,
that a critical mass of matter will explode
but who designed that fact - why not a
millennium or two before, or after,
or a trillion tons or more, required to prime the
Bang?

A formulae by careful design created all the
universe
but what divine inspiration perfected that
concoction
and chose the relativity beyond all theory?

Let us reflect on time:
they tell us, sadly, that we'll never
travel faster than the speed of light -
for if we do we will travel backwards down the path of time.
But here's the flaw to that:
if it takes a hundred thousand years
for light to penetrate
the centre of our universe - that's now.
When the universe was smaller than it is today
the relative effect of time was less,
so early life could travel to and fro,
in and out of time, if their machines could break their gravity's pull,
like spacemen do today.
Its speculation that in some corner of the universe
a billion years or two ago real travellers were born.

We've been cool enough
for a billion years for little aliens from outer space to visit us,
and what message did they receive or give?
No cards, or carving can we find
no message indelible on subconscious minds,
so perhaps we're not worth a visit -
but one there came, it seems unnoticed,
yet with tremendous implication.

The Bang and time and space are all definable.
We, as men, now seem to know or we can learn
yet only one - held all of this in his palm before that Bang,

and He was God and through his son -
predicted and announced,
though few his message heard,
for like all phenomenums,
few ever grasped or understand the Word.

For it is this:-
Our purpose, time and space and life
is in the Word, as John the Gospel writer did reveal,
yet few a study make,
compared with all our sciences, research and trials.
For all this tampering and delvings just result
in moving the fence around mankind's cottage garden,
a little further out,
but no man can make a robin's chest or roses blush
that permanent mystery should be enough
for all God's creatures, such as us.

Our Life

You'll always be the girl I knew, before,
even if time has past and now I'm old,
not you, for you can never be,
you're so indelible on my memory.

That Cardin dress - the bucket shies
all those little moments of the past
that have grown into lifetimes marks.

Marks that are stable, strong,
have stood the test of time
and strengthened -
as our lives together lengthened.

Jerusalem

(an early morning visit to the Holy Sepulchre
reciting the Rosary)

We called Our Lady in Jerusalem,
at early light, down hollow streets,
our muffled feet were background to our voices' ring.
'Hail Marys' echoed in sparse lit alleys of the darkened
souk.

Our gentle pilgrim band
followed in obedience to their leader's bidding,
as corners, along a winding way, became numberless
and the hardened stones harsh, beneath our sandalled feet.

A pause at each sorrowful mystery marked our route
as if a net, and we were fish, was thrown from above
to capture us all for Him.

And then a little square and steps
and that high entrance to the Holy Sepulchre,

so dark inside but, at its right hand post,
a flight to where the Franciscan sits.

Speckled doves pecked the foundation rock
on which, for centuries, the Basilica had stood
while all inside the Orthodox had taken power
and from the dome festoons of hanging lamps
and smoke imposed their culture.

Our Mass was subdued and proper,
in the dim of the great interior church.
Protecting Galgotha and the tomb
from successive centuries of weather, eyes
and infidel destruction.

I doubt I'll see it all again
but memory will not mellow down my recollections,
as reverence, awe and love swept through my mind
and, I trembled as at that final Gate I'll stand,
and pray that it may be ajar for me and all those on
earth I love,
so that our end will be in living light
far from the dark, unhappy, Holy Sepulchre.

Outside the sun had risen higher
and, as a group we hailed to Mary once again
with joyous steps and sound, our backs to agony
and all that darkened misery, torture, Cross and tomb.
Our entreaty loud to Mary
"please pray for us sinners now
and at the moment of our death".

On Reading "In the Footsteps of St. Paul" by H.V. Morton

O what illustrative gift of words
could, by such neat formation,
give out a picture, message and a history,
all drawn as one, upon a canvas of mans memory.

And now I know of St. Paul and all his journeyings,
can smell the smoke of camel dung
in the fires of his imagination.
What else but deeper faith can his words teach me,
nothing is greater than knowing more of truth.

✿ ✿ ✿

The Artist

How can my little touch add beauty to God's world?
Does my freewill give me freedom to add more?
But what can I add that is not His already?
Only myself, my heart, my soul.
For these He gave me.

✧ ✧ ✧

Reality

Through this changing mask that is my face
my mind and heart transmit a little of themselves,
It is a mix of smiling life, yet oft,
of harshness from the pain within.

Is the face the honest reflection of our being
or is it just a form of flesh and bone?
Once fresh and maybe lovely but later,
just flab and ugly.
Does not the mind and maybe heart,
continue to progress
but face and body just regress,
so that all our magnificent thoughts and loves and dedications
just as they bloom are lost in facial degradations.

✧   ✧   ✧

Time Valuable

Exclusive, untouchable, centre of life,
how unlike man's daily world,
yet entwined in every moment.
Time is ceaseless, beyond man's understanding,
for him all tangible things decay, as do mountains
and human thoughts just fade away.
Yet time goes on,
its another grace from God,
elevating Him from man.

For we depend on time to fuel our brief existence,
we devour time as our bread and drink,
without time we are not here.
For God has all the time and, for our breathing life,
has given us our part.

To us time becomes at first irrelevant,
when we have more than we can use,
but when our little lives runs out of time
and cease work, growth, sleep
and all those actions of our own free will,
then we have consumed our allocated share.
And so our conscious mind must learn to know the
value of our time,
before its scarce measure goes
and we go down the narrow tunnel to our trial.

Reflections

Did I make my dreams come true
or did I stop too soon along the way?
No more for me a public-famous seat
but warm and family life - retreat!
Once upon a time for me,
I wanted all that I could see,
my power I did not understand,
loved land and things held in my hand.
Security was number one,
but I'd toss it all upon the wheel
and risk to grasp a million deal.

Gamble, you might call it that,
but all the time, I was in on that.
Only once I passed the reigns
and paid the price of failures pains.
So now I build upon the family
and try to help with full humility
and play a smaller field and give my time and life,
tell all I know of pain and strife,
to those around who need to know
to save their need to plant and in exhaustion, hoe.

Of all I sought I did obtain, but now the last and
greatest of them all - the peaks I see,
in glorious, sweeping steep country.
Where greatness comes from passing on
and leaving, loving, gifting all,

with strings that make life not too easy
and provide still satisfaction to create,
and sow that same seed into theirs,
that they too will find it not too easy
but have room for dreams of all their own,
and with God's good grace within them all,
they have a spark to make a fire
and spirit, strength and hope: to constantly aspire.

❖   ❖   ❖

Life Is Short

Lifetime is so short
and all the Angels say
"but what did you expect
that God would give you men
more than a day
to savour his abundance?"
And if you live above three score years and ten
remember that, as the angels say,
"it is a privilege to live
amongst His men."

The Sensor of Compostela

In human majesty a Bishop spoke,
resounding in the columned beauty
of the sculptured whole
and eight men in crimson capes,
knotted well a cable thick as a strong mans arm,
to a sensor gold.
And with great strength all pulled
the massive weight aloft
and it began to swing with each slow ascending tug
and at the roof, of twenty metres high,
it was horizontal with the floor
and all its sweet devil driving scent,
descended full length upon each aisle
from northern narthex passing alter high
and captured all for Christ
and made ready for His Apostolic Priest.

Waiting For Retribution

How patient has been the Lord to allow us men to poach His earth,
to take all that we desired for just a little trying.
Whatever we want is given and few give thanks.
None speak that this will ever end, as if all earthly joy will last forever.
Riches, beauty and great comfort are in so many places found
and we have the power to talk
and hear across the world,
we dominate the globe as if it all was ours.

But this cup of earthly joy has slopped over into a garden of destruction,
as distant men, in thirst and desolation, remain in pain, unseen, unloved and unacknowledged.
No brother, wanting, is given time;
not every sister, with her child, receives protection.
The headlong flight to luxury and exuberance
devours us all and those in want have no connection.

But surely a price for all this taking will be extorted:
there is a global justice, a levelling of scales.
Is not the historic message plain to see?
Did not Jerusalem, gold-rush towns and trading cities of all times,
lose their shine, decline and prosperity moved on?

Phoenicians, Greeks, Romans are all gone,
we too were once so great we ruled the sea,
but, because it's quiet now and seeming calm,
does it mean that we will never pay the price?
As if the inn keeper will never present the bill -
I think not, He will come again as returns the tide.

✿   ✿   ✿

World War and August

Its August again, but on another sixty years,
as media news renews for me,
but recounts afresh for most,
the history of those desperate years,
when men, in honours name, marched out
and fought for England.

At twelve, I was too young,
yet solid, strong and unafraid.
At eighteen, which was slow and painful in its coming,
it was too late for me to fight for home or country,

as when I donned that longed-for uniform,
both VE and VJ days had passed -
into the new worlds history.

The colour in which I was clad
was not the blue that meant I'd fly
for all the glamour of the air was spent
and now, if there was demand for me at all,
it was for soldiers feet to occupy
what other men had won.

So as a child I watched the war
and, as it happens, did a full mans job
for bombs on vital targets struck,
sudden, silent rockets, flying bombs, robotic power,
shattered homes and England's flower,
and tore our potential strength, burst and blasted,
factories, trains, and damaged hard
the equipment of our fighting strength.
So, in unidentifiable ways,
they slowed us down and bullets,
shells and our retaliation reduced its pace
and that gigantic spirit of our national race, once fired,
was made to pause, before defiance flung
full force, our rightful message at the Hun.

The little job, at my young age,
first was to pass papers round the town,
unknown messages, I carried and
London, in it's war time sin and glory, I got to know.

Its fighting glamour, an artists palate of coloured
uniforms, and notables, De Gaulle and Smuts,
I passed upon my daily round,
St James Park, Pall Mall and Downing Street were on my beat,
their golden pavements beneath my feet.

The dear London I began to love
and I've never lost that adoration
as the history of its trenchant peoples
became revealed through towers and steeples.
The brick and stone of Churchill's throne
were styles so mixed by architrix
that all the past lived on for me
as, in my little present,
I walked the routes of Empire builders,
letting all the past engrave my memory
from it's architectural plenty.

Through osmosis my love was born of London
then out of it did grow my patriotic passion for my Land.
Its simple goodness, beauty, courage,
determined peoples from soil and office, factories, shops and homes
united in one great final conquest of the English Peoples to win the war.

Traditional barriers of colour, class and gender
began their first decay and,
it was then that life, as its become today,

began its metamorphosis.
The war was the chrysalis stage
for our irreligious lives, as from its shell
we did emerge unrecognisable people,
jealous of each others wealth, individualistic, and,
despite the painful victory, less patriotic than before.
A merge of men and women rather drab and
uniform, all dressed up in high new fashion but none
exclusive as before.

Those nights of war were called the blitz
and at sunset all would go
beneath the ground to shelter from the bombs
and shrapnel from our own home guns.
The shrill scream of descending bombs
made men, women, children equally afeared
and then the crash, the dust,
the dark, the breath let out
the cries of fear as yet another fell
and, although for me unheard, the human cries of
agony and pain.
For some, impossibly trapped beneath the wreckage,
the crackle of creeping fire from gas,
first to torture their conscious minds until,
unquenchable flames, devoured their living flesh.
The flying daggers of spiteful glass,
cut eyes and cheeks
and did thrust deep into living bodies,
life was slowly crushed from limbs and lungs and
hearts by weight of shattered buildings.
So this new loathsome form of war,

all the citizens of Europe suffered -
but no real victory won,
only monstrous ruin, death and pain,
full spent to an inglorious conclusion.
No victory, and, for sure no conquest gained
'twas just the realisation, I fear for just one
generation, that war was blind.

It's the space of time that tests indelibility
and plumbs the depth of truth,
buried in the hearts of men.
So we must ask will that time return and will man
ever discover his own futility,
will he grasp that realisation that he is not alone in
this one universe.
That God is not for scorn, and 'tis His love that
reveals what man calls science.
The century of war inspired the search for technical
progress with great success
but mislead man's minds to think that it was he who
owns omnipotence.

And, during lonely war, I thrust on,
and become a grown youth
with all men gone away I could make things happen:
buildings restore, make factories work again
do all the things reserved for grown men in years
gone by.
I discovered my own chemistry and science,
and what I was, but Britain only changed and did
not find itself.

So a soldier I eventually became and
journeyed to the jade green East, and loved even more
my God's own world
and, with vast promotion for my age,
I lowered down the flag on our past triumphs,
we no longer had the strength to rule
and I surrendered sovereignty to bright-eyed Asians
eager for the reins and they became independent.

My instinct, logic, second nature made me assume my
God's great existence but education at war,
deprived me of much, especially so of Him,
until the dawning came to me,
a logical and eventual grasp of truth,
my mind realised the presences of a great creator.
Despite the agony in life and harsh reality of men,
we are tempered, as in a furnace and made to suffer
punishment until repentance dawns.
Life is but a training
and a testing ground for our free will.

So is the inevitability of war a logical conclusion?
And if it is, is it a punitive suffering imposed by God?
Or the inevitable outcome of mankind's selfish
progress?

When all positive steps to hide God's existence have
been taken will events reach collision course again.
Down the ages war and conflict have marked man's
fitful progress
and as the memory of its pain does ebb away

so again come successive,
unthinking and unrealising generations,
with naivety, to display unnatural ignorance of God
and fully hold belief in their own invincible prowess.

In sixty years little wars have punctuated each decade
all vast for those engaged – but yet not global
and, as memory of World War fades
I am fearful of the lack of God in all our lives
as only with Him in the centre of all our minds
will we discover the endless peace His love provides
and escape the hell and pain of yet another war.

✿ ✿ ✿

Wales and Brecon

Poor beauty in rain scarred hills
I now have seen your dramatic lines,
not walked but trundled o'er their sudden edges
and felt the awesome sadness of your land -
gentle, poor and riven.

I knelt a while in Brecon Church-Cathedral,
touched by sturdy columns, not fine drawn,
but in the shortened nave,
a sudden drawing of my eye, took my conscious
mind from altar, candles and the glass
to lists of names enamelled onto brass.

Fathers and the sons of Border men were written there.
Generations of men who died
for Queen and Country and some for Him, who,
like them too, was killed by men.
Although I knelt and prayed, between my fingers
I could count the columns of the names,
in each, at least two hundred,
altogether eleven hundred.
I thought: another World War One,
called Great when I was just a newborn son,
but when I rose to read the caption
these were men who died in bloody action
from Zulu spear, not of my century
but an earlier age than mine - in 1879
And I staggered that I did not know before
the heavy loss this tragic land had suffered,
that so many unknowingly, had died from here
to retain more foreign wealth for England.

And dazed, I wandered down the aisle
and then I saw another list,
again on brass and plain to see,
enshrined 600 more.
Not so many mature men to go out then,
to die in European mud,
from orders, veiled in patriotism,
to fight invaders for
the privilege they called freedom.

And so, still dazed and low, I wandered on
and yet a third list hit my eye

and there, again on enamelled brass but longer now
those fallen, when I was just too young to go.

Another 1,000 border men and some from Warwick,
all cold, a pile of empty soulcases
that for about a score of years were human men.

The realisation was swift and brought tears,
that from these wet and stricken hills
three generations of ploughmen, shepherds, fathers,
had, like valueless wild flowers been gathered,
yet still new, dropped dead,
as if more would endlessly flower again
to be cropped by central government men.

�   ✧   ✧

The Australian Property Unit Trust
(APUT)

They didn't want to back a Pom,
at least not at their own game,
and in their own country.
Battlefields were different places where
blind obedience was easy.

But a Property Trust run by a Pom
was hard.
It would probably be brilliant
but why can't our guys do it?
How could we sell it if a Pom ran it?
Sure, say he's brilliant, he's a brain,
done it all before in London
but its not the same in Melbourne.

And so they waited for an Aus -
to run one -
and he lost two hundred million.

The Builder

I know I could have been great at something,
even just dancing,
not yacht building or playwriting
they're both new,
but big like international that
becomes historic.
My buildings, save one,
are plain and functional
but then I blame the times and not myself
- it's easier that way.
Writing is what in my dying embers
I shall try
but writers need a lifetime
or consumption in their thirties, to capture fame.

So, what have I concentrated my essence into?
Its been a family -
unique, selfish and beautifully normal and human,
brought up against a background
of rural England of a lost era,
unreal, yet surviving
artificial, yet earthy,
and that adventurous place, Australia,
bright and brilliant,
raw and comfortable,
a place of promise and fulfilment
a haven and provider.
A bit like me!

To Grandchildren -
The World is Yours

People must move with the flow,
not hang about where grandpa was,
-life's on the move - every day's new
like a running brook - not dammed up and forlorn.

Because in centuries past
men heaved coal or smelted brass
we've IT now and past skills have gone
so we, like a river, must move on.

No need to stay behind
because we were born here
maybe we've worked it out-
our survival economy gone

Learn about this amazing earth
go and live where you are worth
a man's or woman's fair days work
from hand or brain or imaginations store
but do not stay because its habit -
easy or a gift - you're worth much more.

South Island, New Zealand

Forest of peaks and low lying mist,
a land by rapid rivers riven
whose ancient Alps did time await
before any man could infiltrate.
Few birds, no mammals, no lake or river life
a special place reserved by God as free from strife?

Polynesians in outrigged craft were the first to come,
at the time when French William conquered our
small island here,
though all the world had men before,
until a millennium ago
New Zealand was a paradise unseen.

As centuries passed Fijians came and in due time,
Captain Cook landed there,
And from that visit so much has changed.
The inhabitants at first bold but tranquil men,
laughed and traded with our crews,
whose musket sticks impressed them most
And thus ensured they stayed good hosts.

A century and a half ago came stronger craft of wood, then steel,
with cattle, sheep and little mammals too
and now brown trout, in glacier waters thrive,
brought from English chalk streams live.

So now they've stocked the land enough
and God's beauty still untouched.
Let us all hope and pray
that ferocious man lets it stay that way.

That

It's age I must learn about
Nothing's better than that
but hard to master the meanings
and then respect the answer from that.

When folly shines through the window
and all is as obvious as that
then its time to stop and question
whether life is just about that.

How could I exist by just longing
and hoping to know about that
but nothing comes easy like longing
and I guess we all know about that.

But what's the real reason for living
and finding the answer for that
is it for helping others and suffering
or is it to be selfish and that.

No its exciting and loving and wonderful
and no one knows more about that
but finding that God's message is visible
then, know its all about that.

Rehearsals

Erratic, standing and shifting,
sitting and staring around,
waiting and watching then someone's laughing
all a bit shy or rather too proud.

That's a rehearsal
all nerves on high tension
until that brief moment of mine
and then I know, that all the suspension,
was training of voice to perfection on time.

✧   ✧   ✧

My Secret

How fast they go my days
now I'm near the summit,
that way of life, that each of us must climb.
I'm fit and ready for the most I do,
but secretly, decline.

❖   ❖   ❖

Ancient Oceans

Before the first millennia intrepid sailors,
frail ships and masters,
crossed the seas that none had ever known
and tested out their Makers power
in seeming endless ocean.
They sought to find unknown shores, remove long
mysteries, test rumours and,
in inevitable consequence, developed skills:
to sail, construct and navigate and stretch their
growing, independent wills.

Rulers, Courts and powerful men extracted gain from
all of this, advanced the quality of our lives and
fostered relationships of lasting value cross the world.
It was a bed for seeds of fellowship and love for
universal man and some did flower.

The arts and craftsmanship of others, at one glance,
become delight and challenge too, that all should learn
to better their native artistry and skills
and from such competition greater benefits then flowed
intended for the progress of all mens lives.

And so its been from distant time,
reaching to our daily world
much great beauty, massive wealth and power
yet degradations been always there
short life and early infant death.
The beauty marred by harsh reality

of unequal shares on equals heads,
to easy death, in rat run shanties,
now linked so close, by modern flights,
to excesses beyond mans need, to luxury and
pampered life.

Now so close: yet unseen,
shrugged away as not for me.
How can we kindle mankind's nature
to recognise his starving neighbour.
What must we do to spread our affluence
to struggling lives,
all beneath that single dome of sky that's meant for all,
so all enjoy the gifts with which this special planet is
endowed, with all men working close, as one,
in global unity and shared abundance.

As God had given mankind freedom
to test His mysteries
now pray we all that this same gift of will
be trained and moulded into richer understanding,
tolerance and generous giving
and to the skill that conquered ancient seas
we may, with grace - add love.

Spring Time 2002

Springtime is nativity -
all emerges from dear natures womb,
sprouts and, charged with sudden energy, life grows.
The sky dawns sharp and colours change to brightness.

This spring is better still
as loving sun gives shining hours, so rare for us,
and heavens blue envelopes countryside
and gaily bids farewell to serious winter.

Then in their order, awaiting each their ordained turn,
wild flowers in annual quick succession bloom.
First snowdrops with fairy dignity protrude their
lantern heads,
followed by rival yellow primroses, daffodils and all
those laughing dancers.

But then they fade,
though few brave primroses still invade
the paths of ancient woodland
like remnants of a retreating army that will not give up.

There's columbine with elegance and smiles,
then dominating dandelion attempts to smother all
with vulgar gold
forgiven only when their puff departs.

And now its May the celandine,
cranesbill blue and sometimes pink,

on ancient pastures spread and link,
to live their life, a chaplet long,
midst daisies, campions and spring birds song.
A changing carpet, woven by dear natures love
that we may know that Gods above.

✿   ✿   ✿

Michael's Speech:
Wintershall Nativity Play

The divinity of stars and angels lead the kings and
shepherds to our Lord.
And, in that moment of their understanding,
the instinctive nature of their hearts,
beckoned their minds to realise
the glory laid before their eyes.
For sage and shepherd the wonder was the same,
equal for station, wealth and brain:
our God had come to earth to save His people.

His incarnation here, as man,
created the human world anew,
We are now new washed, new born,
new people living in forgiven time.

Did He make us in his own image
that He might visit us on earth,
to show our human race how we should live?
"Love your God and love your neighbour"
was His great commandment,
And did He also chose to come to show us truth,
to teach us love, bring peace, show proof.

But love is an over spoken word that holds so much
and is, so oft, a smaller meaning meant.
Respect and dignity to all He did include,
obedience to God (and government is also part)
but giving, sharing, comforting and kindness,

unseen and silent that's the loving art,
not softness on a trivial face or passing smile -
followed by forgetfulness.

Forgiveness is also love
that we should never hold a grudge,
distain, despise or labour with a hurt
for these do twist and numb our minds
and stress and make turmoil of our heart.

Yet love is not just for family and those in love with us
but to those unknown.
Those who do not demand;
those daunted, broken hearted and in need of time to
find a life anew;
those in pain and from their loved ones parted.
Equality and truth are love: not jealousy, not envy:
for He is in every face,
the poor, the weak and in us too,
that we may have the heart to love our enemy.
For we must dedicate our time to the slow,
the difficult, the blind.
And, if we fail - fail not because we tried too little -
but because we were not wise enough.
If we have tried; then we will have a place in heaven -
if we have tried, exerted all our strength,
be it great or minor it matters not our bests extent,
so long as we have tried, with love, to emulate God's
son, then - we have loved.

Reflections on Spring

Are violets mauve?
Are bluebells blue?
Whatever colour comes to you?
For some are paler
and some are strong
Who can tell midst all that throng
of beauty, wild and nodding blooms
columbine, campion's and oxcrane's hues.

✧   ✧   ✧

My Life of Goodbyes

Parting is never a joy,
for certainty is not for sure,
as life meanders down its way
who can know the course of every day.
I know the deep and cutting pain
that I might not see them all again.
It's said that character is made of this,
that strength does grow out of loss of bliss,
that life, if stretched, brings out the best
but all I know, that all my life, I've had to say
goodbye.

And now - in age - it's still the hell
of when still young I went away,
to tread those foreign places, foreign tents,
in search of constructive, creative work,
that for my tribe a triumph brought.

But it was always goodbyes of pain
because I might never meet them all again.

Jesus Today

If Jesus were to come again today
would he be as he was before,
the leader of a new life's way
beyond and deeper than the Law.

Would the message from His heart
Be just as it was then
or would it be adapted to this century's style of men.
Would we know he spoke to us
and not from customs out of touch.

At the time of Roman rule and primitive sin,
His message lifted human hearts,
though ignorance and suffering had grown deep,
love burst open and produced a Christian faith.

The message taught to eleven men
has grown to a billion now
and although not here - across the world,
it grows, that ancient need of love,
that is the same today, as it was then,
for he comes each day to fill our empty hearts.

God's Voice

You must know, my son, that which I have proclaimed
and that which I have ordained.
I proclaimed the order of the universe,
first the power of gravity
from suns and planets, moons and stars.
And so there followed light and darkness,
growth, decline,
all life began, blossomed and withered,
that new life could beget itself beyond my constant
attention.

But man I ordained in my own image,
identified his living soul
and the hairs upon his lifetime's head,
but yet I freedom gave to him
that he could choose between right and wrong.

Alaska 1996

A Little History

I didn't grow above my knees
but hips on up I took my share
and now at maturity, in every way,
I stand my ground, advance, am sound.

It was because the early Thirties broke a chain,
no trade, a slump, no economic gain.
My beloved father worked so hard
but could not guard
our future safety, hope or food
and so for several terms, I ate a little less,
no fuss for me, it always was the best,
but now I know why I did not grow
- above my knees.

✣ ✣ ✣

Future Peril

I read that Asia's people
are now sixty per cent of all the world;
That's striking, but what is more
half of them are young.
So young that they are childless yet
but soon their numbers will explode,
and better that than some destroying bomb.

But our exquisite life and
safety will become a dream
for when they populate above three quarters
their God given rights of light and
food and safety too,
will impinge on us - how overdue?

And so we soft and still self nurturing,
have every need to heed the sign,
that's now rising in the economic sky
for we have lapsed beyond our Christian faith:
forgotten love
and now must return to all that's in His teachings
feed the hungry, heal the sick,
remember the meek
for - as we know - they will inherit
and better, by far, that we share our
globe with generous magnanimity
than we force them to seek us out
with sword and fiery dragon.

Recollections

Brian Kelly was a Brave,
dark, tall and silent,
handsome and Red Indian,
except we sat together at school
and his image was like my hero - a Mohican.
We raced and flirted with the girls,
worked hard and laughed,
neither really knew the war -
on BBC and very serious -
so a little nationalism was sparked
and fighting seemed glamorous -
but we didn't know.

He was more than a year older
but I kept up - I did not realise the prize that I
possessed.
And so he went first to fight
and I forgot him as I began to work in London's
war.
At night the bombs had fallen round our Square
caused a thrill, frustration - hate
and so I longed to fight - retaliate
and prove that I too could be a man.

A man - as if to fight was that,
To kill? defend? enjoy? I did not know?
But all my cousins - one captured, one crashed one

fighting still,
were doing that.

But Brian went first and died.
On some French beach - bullet, bomb, mine?
I know not but he is not here now.
Another manboy, his name was Roy
slightly older still, was shot down.
He bombed the u-boat pens at Brest
and was with those
who failed to return at dawn.

What a long time ago for some -
but recent, fresh in memory still for me,
as youthhood never goes away
and first experiences linger on for ever.

A Little Prayer

Jesus my Father do you exist
Jesus my Father do you know me
Jesus my Father do you care about me
Jesus my Father do you love me.
I know you do.

✧ ✧ ✧

Santiago de Compostela
The Classic Choir of the European Union

Sharp air and a low grey mist covered
the holy guest of a thousand years.
Lying shallow, beneath the alter.
Saint James, a kinsman of our Christ,
interred from Egypt in unknown times
lies now enshrined with faithful servant,
followers and friends,
on this far European ocean edge.
His bones, encased in silver blessed
and his mortal image cast in stone above our head.

And so to pray so many pilgrims gathered
with hope of grace for their great travellings.
Such masonry, so worked, is rare, even at this late date,
as towers and fenestration,
arches and slim columns share, in striking glory,
the golden lichen gilded there.

In scarlet cap and flowing robes,
a Holy cardinal appears
and in that vast culture of art and stone,
resounds, as only Cardinals can do.
And then a choir,
a decade from each European nation,
does swell in rapturous single sound,
vibrating pillars, aisle and ornament
as human harmony joins stone and age
in glorious love and Godly praise.

Just as our Lord rose to eternal life in that first all
forgiving Eucharist,
the prayers of present men joined with those of
centuries gone,
soaked into ancient stone and saturated saintly forms,
Our Lady's figure, angels and of holy men.
And pilgrims, tourists and many other earthly beings,
resounded in prayer and song - sheer human joy -
as swinging sensor, gold and heavy
that, on that day,
eight men did swing above the northern window
and frighteningly rush down towards those faithful
heads that did not see
since Jesus stole their hearts in praying ecstasy.

To My Sons

I have to ask -
Are you sorry for talking to me like that?
or has your life been so trying? I think not,
but know the inherited anxiety you wear upon your
brow.

May I say that over reaction is a personal trait.
Why did I leave Britain in my prime
to transfer my drive and talents to a better place?
It was not over reaction but destiny that made me go,
I only knew the pain.

I did not want those I loved to suffer,
but now, if you must, you must go
and inherit that over self reaction.

But yet I went, sold all and went away
into an unknown dangerous world
with responsibilities too heavy - almost to carry -
my love for you and all my tribe
made me go so you would all survive.

So my life and yours, so far
have not been 'just the same',
the pain, in heart and mind
and even personal frame
paid dearly for the litigious, economic strain
that has been, but just for me - my life.
The total risk of all upon one deal

and wanting so much the safety and enough security
that I could sleep and preserve upon the faces
of my wife and all my children - serenity.

A man is responsible for his wife's face,
and then his own so, if it,
towards the end is hard and stark
no love, no warmth or glow
then all has failed
but if a little love protrudes the mask
and though, for a lifetime hidden from the world,
the real face shines,
then all in heaven and earth will safely be.

So, if you want to go into a turbulent life,
no time at home,
because you believe that it is the best for you and yours
And between the crests and troughs of frequent
economic cycles
you are prepared to sacrifice yourself for yours
then you must leave this fold and try and make another.

Or if you want to hold
the old man's arms aloft like Moses,
and direct this battlefield yourself with him,
and in the end make this fold a home
for yours and all the others then please stay
and integrate wholeheartedly with us.
But if you need to go and do your own construction
Remember I've been there and,
for you, will always here remain to help
until God takes me.